Presented to:

Danielle Manning

by:

Alex, Diane &
Charlene Morales

•••

John 3:16

My First Prayer:

My First Bible Memory Verse:

My First Words about Jesus:

My First Step Bible

by
MACK THOMAS

Illustrated by
EDWARD GLEN FRENCH

MY FIRST STEP BIBLE

© 1992 by Questar Publishers, Inc.

Second Printing, 1992

My First Step Bible is printed in both
pink-cover and blue-cover editions

Pink-Cover Edition: ISBN 0-945564-49-X
Blue-Cover Edition: ISBN 0-945564-48-1

PRINTED IN MEXICO

Questar Publishers, Inc.
Post Office Box 1720
Sisters, Oregon 97759

19 Old Testament Stories...

God Made Our World!—6

The First Man and Woman—8

Safe on a Boat—10

A Man Chosen by God—12

A Dream about Heaven—14

A Beautiful Coat—16

A Man Forgives—18

A Baby in a Basket—20

A Burning Bush—22

Escape through the Sea—24

Food in the Desert—26

God's Good Rules—28

The Walls Fall Down—30

A Voice in the Night—32

A Boy Who Killed a Giant—34

A Man Fed by Birds—36

Alive in a Furnace of Fire—38

Alive in a Lions' Den—40

Three Days in a Fish's Belly—42

26 New Testament Stories...

This Baby Is God's Son—44

Shepherds and Angels—46

Following a Star—48

Finding a Missing Boy—50

A Voice from Heaven—52

Following Jesus—54

Jesus Stops a Storm—56

A Little Girl Is Alive Again—58

Little Becomes Much—60

Walking Across the Sea—62

Light on a Mountain—64

A Story of Kindness—66

A Story of Love—68

A Dead Man Comes Alive—70

God Loves Children—72

A Blind Man Now Can See—74

A Little Man in a Tree—76

Jesus in Jerusalem—78

Jesus Suffers and Dies—80

Jesus Is Risen from the Dead!—82

Jesus Goes Back to Heaven—84

Sharing Everything—86

A Blinding Light—88

An Angel Rescues Peter—90

Singing in Jail—92

Jesus Will Take Us to Heaven—94

GOD MADE OUR WORLD!

Before God made our world, everything was dark and empty. Then God said, "Let there be light"—and there *was* light!

So God made the first day and night.

On the second day, God made the sky. The third day, He brought water together to make oceans, and He made dry ground. He covered the ground with trees and grass and flowers.

God saw that everything He made was good.

from the OLD Testament:

On the fourth day, God made the sun and moon and stars. The fifth day, He made fish to fill the ocean, and birds to fill the sky. The sixth day God made animals, and He made people —just like you and me. It was all so very good. And on the seventh day...God rested.

- *Here's Something for Your Heart:* Who made the world and the people all around me? God did!

- *And Here's Something You Can Pray:* Thank You, God, for making everything so good.

THE FIRST MAN AND WOMAN

Adam and Eve were the first man and woman. God made them, and gave them a garden to live in and take care of. In their beautiful garden they had everything to eat, and everything to see and enjoy. They were happy.

But one day, Adam and Eve disobeyed God. They ate the one and only thing which God told them never to eat.

Now they were unhappy and afraid.

from the OLD Testament:

God came walking in the garden, and He said to Adam and Eve, "What have you done?" They told Him what they did.

So God punished them. They had to leave the garden and never go back. An angel with a sword of fire would not let them go back in.

- *Here's Something for Your Heart:* We can't be happy when we disobey God.

- *And Here's Something You Can Pray:* Help me, Lord, to remember what is right and do it.

ADAM & EVE (Genesis 2:4—3:24)   **9**

SAFE ON A BOAT

Many more people were born into the world, and they did more and more bad things. Everyone was bad—everyone except Noah. Noah and his family obeyed God.

God said, "Noah, I am going to destroy all these bad people with a flood of water. So build an ark to put your family in. Build it big enough to hold two of every kind of animal, too. Your family and the animals will be safe."

from the OLD Testament:

Noah built the ark, and put his family and the animals inside. God shut them in. It rained forty days and nights, flooding the world with water. But everyone in the ark was safe.

God dried up the flood-water, and put a rainbow in the sky. And Noah gave thanks to God.

- *Here's Something for Your Heart:* God is able to protect everyone who loves and obeys Him.
- *And Here's Something You Can Pray:* Thank You, God, for keeping me safe.

A Man Chosen by God

"Can you count all the stars in the sky?" That's what God asked Abraham one night.

Abraham was God's friend. God promised Abraham lots of children, and children for those children, and more children for those— as many children as there are stars in the sky.

Abraham and his wife Sarah were old, and they did not have even one little boy or girl. But Abraham still believed God's promise.

from the OLD Testament:

And God *kept* his promise. When Sarah and Abraham were very old, they had a baby boy. They named him Isaac. Through Isaac, and Isaac's children, and their children, Abraham became the father of many, many sons and daughters—as many as the stars in the sky.

- *Here's Something for Your Heart:* When God makes a promise, He *keeps* it!

- *And Here's Something You Can Pray:* Dear God, please help me keep the promises I make.

ABRAHAM (Genesis 15, 17, 18, 21)   **13**

A Dream about Heaven

Jacob was one of Isaac's children. He was now a grown-up man. He was on a long trip, and he was going all by himself.

When the sun went down, Jacob stopped for the night. He found a rock to use for a pillow. He went to sleep, and had a dream. He saw steps going up from earth to heaven. Angels were going up and down the steps. And high at the top was God Himself.

When Jacob woke up, he asked God to take care of him on his long trip.

And God did just that. Jacob went to a place where he kept sheep and goats. He later became a rich man. He got married, and had thirteen children—one girl and twelve boys.

- *Here's Something for Your Heart:* God is in heaven, but He takes care of His children here on earth.

- *And Here's Something You Can Pray:* Lord God, please take good care of me when I grow up.

A Beautiful Coat

When Jacob was an old man, his son Joseph was born. Jacob loved Joseph and gave him a coat that had many beautiful colors.

Joseph dreamed that someday he would be a leader over his ten older brothers. He told his brothers about this dream, and they didn't like it. In fact, one day they took off his coat of beautiful colors, and they threw Joseph down into a dark, empty hole.

Some men came by on camels. Joseph's brothers pulled him out of the hole, and they sold him for money to those men. They let the men on camels take Joseph far away.

Joseph's brothers thought they would never see him again. But they were wrong.

- *Here's Something for Your Heart:* If we have sisters or brothers, God wants us to be kind to them.

- *And Here's Something You Can Pray:* Lord, help me to be kind to everyone in my family.

A MAN FORGIVES

Joseph was taken to Egypt as a slave-boy. There he grew into a wise and strong and handsome man. One day he was thrown into jail, though he had done nothing wrong. God took good care of Joseph, and helped him get out of jail.

The king of Egypt saw how wise Joseph was, and he made him a leader. Joseph was no longer a slave. Joseph's job was to make sure everyone in Egypt had enough food to eat.

from the OLD Testament:

Where Joseph's brothers lived, there was very little to eat. So they came to Egypt to buy food. And there they found Joseph!

Joseph hugged and kissed his brothers. He forgave them for what they did to him when he was a boy. And he gave them lots of food.

- *Here's Something for Your Heart:* God is pleased when we forgive others.

- *And Here's Something You Can Pray:* Forgive me, God, for the wrong things I have done to others.

A Baby in a Basket

The Hebrews were the children of Abraham.
They were God's special people. They lived in
Egypt, but the king of Egypt tried to kill their
baby boys. So when baby Moses was born, his
mother put him in a little basket-boat. She hid
the basket in some reeds at the edge of the
river. Moses' big sister was watching the basket
to see what would happen next.

And this is what happened:

from the OLD Testament:

The princess of Egypt—the king's daughter—
came down to wash in the river. She saw the
baby in the basket-boat, and heard him crying.

Then she took him home with her to live.
Moses grew up in the palace of the king. But he
never forgot about God and God's people.

- *Here's Something for Your Heart:* God has big
  plans for all His people—even babies!

- *And Here's Something You Can Pray:* Thank You,
  Lord, that I can be part of Your special people.

A BURNING BUSH

What's this? A bush on fire? And yet the bush never burns up!

Moses saw the bush. He was a man now. He was living in the desert. He had run away from Egypt.

Suddenly, Moses heard the voice of God in the burning bush. "My people are sad," God said. "They are slaves in Egypt. Moses, I want *you* to lead my people out of Egypt."

from the OLD Testament:

Moses went with his brother, Aaron, to talk to the king of Egypt. "You must let God's people leave Egypt," Moses told him. "This is what God says: 'Let My people go!'"

And how did the mean king of Egypt answer Moses? Like this: He said, "No!"

- *Here's Something for Your Heart:* Sometimes God speaks to us in surprising ways.
- *And Here's Something You Can Pray:* Help me to be brave when I tell other people about You.

ESCAPE THROUGH THE SEA

Finally, the king of Egypt let God's people go.
But then he changed his mind. He sent soldiers
to catch God's people and bring them back.

God's people came to the edge of the sea.
They had no place to go. The king's soldiers
were right behind them, and all this water was
in front of them. Oh, no! What could they do?

God told Moses to stretch out his hand.
Moses did, and the waters of the sea split open.

from the OLD Testament:

Right through the middle of the sea, there was a road for God's people! They went over to the other side. But the water covered up the king's soldiers when they tried to cross, too.

Safe on the other side, the people of God sang songs, and gave thanks to God.

- *Here's Something for Your Heart:* God can make a dry road right through the middle of the sea!

- *And Here's Something You Can Pray:* Dear God, please keep me and my family safe.

THE EXODUS (Exodus 14)

Food in the Desert

God led His people away from Egypt. He put a tall tower of cloud in the sky to show them which way to go. When the sun went down, the cloud was bright with fire. Moses and all of God's people could see it, day or night.

They followed the cloud into the desert. The desert was dry, with not much water or food.

"What will we drink?" God's people said. God showed them where to find water.

from the OLD Testament:

"What will we eat?" God's people said. So every night, God sent down manna from the sky. What is manna? It was little white pieces of bread, and they tasted like honey cookies.

Every morning, the ground was covered with manna. So everyone had plenty to eat.

- *Here's Something for Your Heart:* God will always show His people what to do and where to go.

- *And Here's Something You Can Pray:* Thank You, God, for giving us the food and water we need.

God's Good Rules

Moses and God's people came to a high mountain in the desert. The mountain was covered with a cloud. There was thunder on the mountain, and lightning and fire and smoke.

God called out to Moses from the mountain: "Come up here!" Moses went up the mountain. God said, "See how I brought all of you out of Egypt! Yes, you are My very own people! And now I will tell you the best way to live."

from the OLD Testament:

Then God gave Moses good rules for the people to obey. He wrote them down on pieces of stone so Moses could show them to everyone. These rules tell God's people how to love God with all our heart. And they tell us how to love one another, too.

- *Here's Something for Your Heart:* In the Bible, God tells us how to love Him, and how to love others.
- *And Here's Something You Can Pray:* Help me love You with all my heart, and to love other people.

THE WALLS FALL DOWN

God's people came to the town of Jericho. God wanted His people to have this town. But soldiers in Jericho wanted to fight God's people and send them away. They were enemies of God's people. They did not worship God.

Jericho had high walls all around it. The soldiers closed the gates tight. No one could go out of the town, and no one could go in.

God told His people exactly what to do.

So they did it. Every day for six days they marched around Jericho's walls, and played horns. On the seventh day they marched again, seven times. Then everyone shouted... and Jericho's walls fell down with a crash!

God's people went inside. Jericho was theirs.

- *Here's Something for Your Heart:* When God wants us to have something, He will help us get it.
- *And Here's Something You Can Pray:* Lord God, I'm glad that You're so strong.

JOSHUA AT JERICHO (Joshua 5:13—6:27)   **31**

A VOICE IN THE NIGHT

Eli woke up. Samuel was standing by his bed.
"Here I am," the boy said. "You called me."

"No, I didn't call you," said Eli. "You can go
back to bed." So Samuel went back to his room.

Eli woke up again, and saw Samuel standing there. "I heard you call me," the boy said.

"No, I didn't call you," said Eli. So Samuel
went back to bed, and Eli went back to sleep.

Once more Eli woke up. There was Samuel!

from the OLD Testament:

"It must be God who is calling you," said
Eli. "If God calls you again, answer Him."

Samuel went back to bed. Then he heard his
name being called: *"Samuel! Samuel!"*

"I'm listening, Lord," Samuel answered.
And that night God told Samuel many things.

- *Here's Something for Your Heart:* God can speak to
  our hearts when we are quiet and listening.
- *And Here's Something You Can Pray:* Thank You,
  Lord, for always being with me, even at night.

A BOY WHO KILLED A GIANT

A boy named David went to visit his older brothers. They were soldiers for the people of God. They were fighting the Philistines.

The Philistines had a terrible giant on their side. His name was Goliath. He kept shouting, "Come fight me!" The soldiers of the people of God were afraid of Goliath.

But David wasn't afraid. He saw Goliath. He heard Goliath say, "Come fight me!"

from the OLD Testament:

David stepped up to fight Goliath. David said, "You have a sword and spear and shield. But I'm on God's side, and God will win." With a sling, David threw a rock, and it knocked Goliath down. Then he stood over Goliath and took away his sword. The giant was dead!

- *Here's Something for Your Heart:* In God's eyes, a giant is no bigger than anyone else.
- *And Here's Something You Can Pray:* Lord, help me to see things the way You see them.

DAVID & GOLIATH (1 Samuel 17)

A Man Fed by Birds

Elijah told the king about God, but the king didn't like it. The king was angry with Elijah.

So God told him where to hide. "You can drink water from the brook there," God said. "And the blackbirds will bring you food."

Elijah went to the place God told him. Blackbirds brought him bread and meat twice a day.

One day Elijah met some people on a mountain. "I'll show you who is God," Elijah said.

from the OLD Testament:

Elijah made a stack of twelve rocks. He put wood and meat on the rocks. And he poured water over all of it. Then Elijah prayed. And God sent down fire from the sky! The fire burned up the meat, the wood, and even the water and the rocks. Only God could do that!

- *Here's Something for Your Heart:* God takes care of us in many different ways.

- *And Here's Something You Can Pray:* Dear Lord, I know that you're my God, and I'm glad You are!

ALIVE IN A FURNACE OF FIRE

The king of Babylon built a huge golden statue. And he said, "Whoever doesn't fall down and worship this statue will be thrown into a furnace of fire." Then someone told the king that three Hebrew men—Shadrach, Meshach, and Abednego—would not bow down to the statue. "We will worship only God," these men said.

The king was angry! He ordered those three men tied up and thrown into the fiery furnace.

from the OLD Testament:

But then the king saw someone in the fire who looked like an angel, walking with the three men. And the men were not burned. They were not even hot! Even their clothes were fine.

When the three men walked out of the fire… the king himself gave praise to God!

- *Here's Something for Your Heart:* God always takes good care of the people who worship only Him.

- *And Here's Something You Can Pray:* Help me, God, to never worship anything or anyone but You.

Alive in a Lions' Den

Look inside that window, and you can see Daniel praying. Daniel loved God, and three times every day he prayed to God on his knees.

One day the king and his helpers made a new law. This law said that anyone praying to God would be thrown into a den of lions.

Did that make Daniel stop praying? No! He still opened his window, got down on his knees, and prayed to God three times every day.

from the OLD Testament:

So the king and his helpers threw Daniel into the lions' den. The lions were hungry, but did they eat Daniel? No! God had sent an angel to keep those lions from biting him.

And when the king saw that Daniel was safe, he made a new law that gave praise to God.

- *Here's Something for Your Heart:* God is pleased when we love Him and pray to Him.

- *And Here's Something You Can Pray:* Thank You, God, for brave heroes like Daniel.

THREE DAYS IN A FISH'S BELLY

Jonah was trying to get away from God. He didn't want to go where God told him to go. Instead, Jonah got on a ship to cross the sea.

But when God sent a terrible storm, the sailors on the ship found out what Jonah was doing. Jonah asked them to throw him into the ocean. And that's just what they did.

Then God caused Jonah to be swallowed by a great fish—maybe it was even a whale!

from the OLD Testament:

Jonah was inside that dark fishy belly for three days and three nights. Jonah was sorry now. He prayed to God, and God made the fish throw up Jonah onto dry ground.

Once again, God told Jonah where to go and what to do. And this time, Jonah *obeyed God.*

- *Here's Something for Your Heart:* We can never run away from God—and besides, why should we?

- *And Here's Something You Can Pray:* Lord God, help me be quick to obey You.

THIS BABY IS GOD'S SON

One day God sent the angel Gabriel to give good news to Mary, a young woman. "Mary," Gabriel said, "God is doing something great for you! You're going to have a baby boy! Name Him Jesus, because He will be God's Son, and God will make Him the King forever!"

An angel also visited Joseph, a man who loved Mary. The angel told him about Mary's baby. "Name Him Jesus," the angel said.

from the NEW Testament:

Joseph and Mary had to take a long trip, to Bethlehem. Bethlehem was crowded, and they had to stay where animals were kept and fed. While they were there, Mary's baby was born. And what did Mary and Joseph name Him? That's right...they called Him *Jesus!*

- *Here's Something for Your Heart:* Jesus is God's Son, and God has made Him our King forever!

- *And Here's Something You Can Pray:* Thank You, God, for sending us Jesus, Your very own Son.

SHEPHERDS AND ANGELS

In the dark of night on a hillside near Bethlehem, some shepherds saw an angel—and a bright light shining all around! They were afraid, but the angel told them not to be.

"I bring great and happy news for everyone," the angel said: "Today a Savior is born to you. He is *Christ the Lord.* You'll find Him wrapped up and lying in a manger." Suddenly the sky was filled with angels praising God.

from the NEW Testament:

When the angels went back into heaven, the shepherds said, "Let's go find the Savior!"

They hurried to Bethlehem. They found Mary and Joseph, and they found Baby Jesus lying in a manger, just as the angel had said.

Then they told everyone what they had seen.

- *Here's Something for Your Heart:* When God sent us His Son Jesus, it was great and happy news!

- *And Here's Something You Can Pray:* Help me to tell others about Jesus, just as the shepherds did.

SHEPHERDS VISIT JESUS (Luke 2:8-20)

Following a Star

From far away in the east, wise men were following a star. They were glad to see it, because they knew why this star was in the sky: The King of God's people had been born!

The wise men wanted to find the new King, and to worship Him.

The star kept moving, and the wise men kept following. Then the star stopped right over the place where Jesus was, in Bethlehem.

from the NEW Testament:

The wise men went into the house, and saw
Jesus with His mother, Mary. They kneeled
down before Jesus, and worshiped Him.

Then they opened their gifts for Him: gold,
which was shiny and bright; and frankincense
and myrrh, which smelled so nice.

- *Here's Something for Your Heart:* When we want to
worship God, He will help us find Him.

- *And Here's Something You Can Pray:* Lord Jesus, I
want to always love You and worship You.

FINDING A MISSING BOY

Where, oh where, could Jesus be?

Mary and Joseph and Jesus had been in Jerusalem with their friends and family. Now they were all on the road going home—all except Jesus. So Mary and Joseph were worried.

Jesus wasn't a baby anymore. He was twelve years old. But where *was* He? Joseph and Mary went back to Jerusalem to look for Him. After three days, they found Jesus in the Temple.

from the NEW Testament:

Jesus was talking with Bible teachers there. They were surprised to hear how much Jesus knew about God. Why did Jesus know so much about God? Because God was His Father!

Jesus went home with Mary and Joseph. He obeyed them, and He grew stronger and wiser.

- *Here's Something for Your Heart:* When Jesus was a child, He loved God and obeyed His parents.
- *And Here's Something You Can Pray:* Help me to grow up strong and wise, just as Jesus did.

A Voice from Heaven

Jesus was now a man, good and wise and strong. He went to the Jordan River. A man who ate grasshoppers and honey was there. His name was John. He told people about Jesus. He told them to do what God says is right. John also baptized people. He baptized them in the water, to show that they wanted to obey God.

Jesus said to John, "Baptize Me, for this is right to do." So John baptized Jesus in the river.

As Jesus came up out of the water, He saw
heaven open. The Spirit of God came upon
Him, like a dove flying down from the sky.

Then God's voice called out to Jesus from
heaven: "You are My Son, and I love You, and
I am very pleased with You."

- *Here's Something for Your Heart:* Jesus always did
  what was right. He never did anything wrong.

- *And Here's Something You Can Pray:* Help me,
  dear Lord, to do what is right.

FOLLOWING JESUS

Jesus was walking by the Sea of Galilee. He saw some men with their boats: Peter and his brother Andrew, and James and his brother John. They were fishermen. With their big nets, they could catch lots of fish.

"Come and follow Me," Jesus said to them. So Peter and Andrew and James and John left their boats and their big fishing nets, and they went with Jesus, wherever He would go.

from the NEW Testament:

Jesus kept walking. He saw Matthew sitting at a table where people paid him money. Jesus said to him, "Follow Me." Matthew got up from the money table and walked away with Jesus.

These men decided to stay close to Jesus. He was their Best Friend and their Teacher.

- *Here's Something for Your Heart:* Jesus is our Best Friend and our Teacher.

- *And Here's Something You Can Pray:* Jesus, I want to follow You. I want to stay close to You!

JESUS STOPS A STORM

Oh, what a storm on the Sea of Galilee! The wind was blowing hard. And waves on the water were crashing and thrashing.

Right in the middle of the storm, Jesus and His friends were in a boat on the sea. Jesus was asleep, but His friends were awake and afraid. Their boat was filling up with water!

"Wake up, Lord, wake up!" they said to Jesus. "We'll surely die in this storm!"

from the NEW Testament:

Jesus looked at the wind and the waves. "Stop!" He said. The storm stopped at once. Just like that, it was over. All was quiet.

"Why were you so afraid?" Jesus said to His friends. "Don't you believe in Me?" Now they understood better that Jesus was God's Son.

- *Here's Something for Your Heart:* When we believe in Jesus, we don't have to be afraid of any storm.

- *And Here's Something You Can Pray:* Lord Jesus, I believe in You. Help me not to be afraid.

CALMING THE STORM (Matthew 8:23-27; Mark 4:35-41; Luke 8:22-25) ▪ **57**

A Little Girl Is Alive Again

A man named Jairus was on his knees before Jesus. "My little girl is dying," he cried. "But if You will come and touch her, she will live." She was twelve years old, and the only little girl this man had.

Jesus went with Jairus. Before they reached his house, some people came and said, "It's too late; She's already dead." But Jesus told Jairus not to be afraid. "Just believe," He said.

from the NEW Testament:

Jesus said to the people, "The girl isn't dead; she's just asleep." But they laughed at Him.

Inside the house, Jesus said, "Little girl, get up!" And she did! She got up and walked around. She was alive again! She was well!

Then Jesus helped get her something to eat.

- *Here's Something for Your Heart:* It's never too late to get help from the Lord.

- *And Here's Something You Can Pray:* Dear Lord, I'm glad I can always come to You for help.

LITTLE BECOMES MUCH

One day, thousands and thousands of people came out in the countryside to see and hear Jesus. Many were sick, but Jesus made them well.

Then it got late. It was time to eat, but almost no one had any food. Among all those thousands of people, there were only five little loaves of bread to eat, and two fish. "Bring the food to Me," Jesus said. He told everyone to sit down, then He thanked God for the food.

He shared the bread and fish with everyone. Suddenly the bread and fish became more… and more…and more…and still more! There was more than enough! In fact, after everyone had eaten and was full, Jesus' friends filled up twelve baskets with the leftovers.

- *Here's Something for Your Heart:* As God takes care of us, He can make a little become a lot.

- *And Here's Something You Can Pray:* Thank You, Lord, that You care about everything I need.

Walking Across the Sea

After Jesus fed all those thousands of people,
He sent them home. And He sent His friends
out in a boat to cross the sea. After He said
goodbye to everyone, Jesus climbed a mountain. And up on that mountain, He prayed.

It was dark now. Out in the middle of the
sea, in the middle of the night, Jesus' friends
were rowing their boat. It was hard, hard
work, for the wind was blowing against them.

from the NEW Testament:

Jesus loved these men. He walked out on the water toward them. When He was close to the boat, they saw Him. At first they thought He was a ghost, and they cried out in fear.

But right away Jesus called out to His friends: "Be brave! It is I; don't be afraid."

- *Here's Something for Your Heart:* We can always be brave if we remember that Jesus is with us.

- *And Here's Something You Can Pray:* Help me to remember how close You always are to me.

JESUS WALKS ON WATER (Matt. 14:22-33; Mark 6:45-52; John 6:16-21) ▬ **63**

LIGHT ON A MOUNTAIN

Being close to Jesus was so exciting for Jesus'
friends! They saw Him make sick people well.
They saw Him make dead people come alive.

But they also heard Him say that someday
He would be killed. "And after three days," He
said, "I will rise up and be alive again."

One day, Jesus climbed another high mountain. With Him were His friends Peter and
James and John. No one else was with them.

from the NEW Testament:

Suddenly, on top of the mountain, light began shining all over Jesus. His face was as bright as the sun. A white cloud came down, and Jesus' friends heard God's voice from the cloud. God said, "This is My Son, and I love Him. Listen to everything He says!"

- *Here's Something for Your Heart:* God tells us to listen carefully to everything Jesus says.

- *And Here's Something You Can Pray:* I'm glad, dear God, that You love Jesus, and that You love me!

A Story of Kindness

This is a story Jesus told:

Once there was a man walking on the road from Jerusalem to Jericho. Suddenly robbers attacked him and hurt him, and took away his clothes. They left him almost dead.

Two other men walked by on the road, but they wouldn't stop to help. Then a stranger came by. "Oh no!" the stranger cried. "This man is hurt!" He quickly began to help him.

from the NEW Testament:

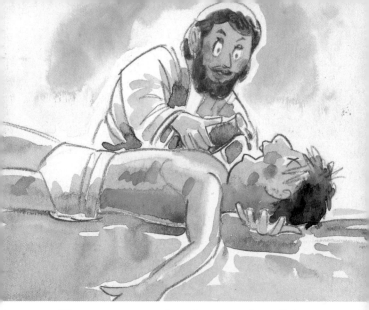

The stranger put bandages and medicine on the man where he was hurt. Then he put the man on his donkey, and took him to a place where he could rest and get better.

The stranger was kind—and Jesus said *we* are to be kind, just as this stranger was.

- *Here's Something for Your Heart:* Whenever anyone is hurt, Jesus knows, and Jesus cares.
- *And Here's Something You Can Pray:* Help me to be kind and caring to those who need help.

A STORY OF LOVE

This is another story Jesus told:

There was a man who had two sons. And one son said, "Father, give me all the money that you were someday going to give me."

So his father gave him the money.

Then the son went away and wasted the money until it was all gone. He got a job feeding pigs. There was food for the pigs, but no food for him. He was very, very sad.

from the NEW Testament:

"I did wrong," he told himself. "I'm going home to tell my father how sorry I am."

When the father saw his son, he ran out and hugged him and kissed him. He gave him new clothes and lots of good food. And he said, "You were lost, my son—but now you're found!"

- *Here's Something for Your Heart:* God is always ready to forgive us for the wrong things we do.
- *And Here's Something You Can Pray:* Father God, I'm glad You love me as Your very own child.

A DEAD MAN COMES ALIVE

Jesus was crying. His good friend Lazarus was dead. Jesus loved Lazarus. Lazarus had two sisters, Mary and Martha. Jesus loved them, too. They were sad, and Jesus cried with them.

"Your brother will rise again," Jesus said to Mary and Martha. "I am the One who can make Lazarus rise from the dead. I am the One who can make him alive again."

He went to a cave where Lazarus lay dead.

Jesus asked some men to roll away the stone from the door of the cave, and they did.

Then Jesus shouted: "Come out, Lazarus!"

Suddenly, Lazarus walked out! He was alive, but he was still wrapped up in grave-clothes.

"Unwrap him," Jesus said, "and let him go!"

- *Here's Something for Your Heart:* With Jesus we can live forever. Jesus makes us alive again.

- *And Here's Something You Can Pray:* Thank You, Lord, that I don't have to be afraid to die.

GOD LOVES CHILDREN

One day, some mothers and fathers brought their children to see Jesus. They wanted Jesus to hold their children, and to pray for them.

But Jesus' friends told the mothers and fathers to go away, and not to bother Jesus.

So Jesus told His friends, "Let those little children come to Me! Don't stop them!" And He said, "God's kingdom belongs to little children such as these."

from the NEW Testament:

Jesus held the children in His arms. He prayed for them, and made them happy.

"I tell you the truth," Jesus said to His grown-up friends: "To enter God's kingdom in heaven, you must receive it as a gift—just as a little child does."

- *Here's Something for Your Heart:* Little children are always at home in God's kingdom.

- *And Here's Something You Can Pray:* Lord Jesus, You are my Friend and my King!

A BLIND MAN NOW CAN SEE

Beside a crowded road one day, a blind beggar heard someone say that Jesus was passing by.

"Jesus, Son of David!" the poor blind man shouted. "Please do something to help me!"

"Oh, hush!" said people around him. But he shouted even louder, and Jesus heard him.

Jesus stopped, and asked the blind man to come to Him. The man jumped up and went to the place where he heard Jesus speaking.

from the NEW Testament:

Jesus said to the blind man, "What do you want Me to do for you?"

"Teacher," said the man, "I want to see!"

"You can go now," said Jesus. "Since you believe in Me, your eyes are now well."

The man opened his eyes. *Yes!* He could *see!*

- *Here's Something for Your Heart:* Jesus is always the One to ask for help.

- *And Here's Something You Can Pray:* Thank You, Lord, that You made my eyes to see.

A Little Man in a Tree

"Zacchaeus, hurry and come down," said Jesus
to a man high up in a sycamore tree. "I'm
going to stay at your house today." Zacchaeus
was in the tree that day because he was short,
and he wanted to see Jesus better. After Jesus
called him, he hurried down from the tree. He
took Jesus to his home, and said, "Welcome!"

Zacchaeus had been taking lots of money
away from other people. They didn't like him.

from the NEW Testament:

So Zacchaeus said to Jesus, "Today I'll give half my money to poor people who need it. And if I've taken money away from anyone I shouldn't have, I'll give him back lots more."

Jesus said, "I know this man has been rescued by God. He belongs in God's family!"

- *Here's Something for Your Heart:* Jesus loves all of us—even the people that other people don't like.
- *And Here's Something You Can Pray:* Thank You, Lord, for loving me.

JESUS IN JERUSALEM

One day Jesus rode a young donkey into the city of Jerusalem. The people were glad to see Him. "Hosanna!" they shouted. *"Hosanna!"*

But soon there was trouble. Some men wanted to catch Jesus and kill Him. Jesus knew all about this, because He knows everything.

One night Jesus had dinner with His friends. He told them He loved them. Their feet were dirty, so He washed their feet.

from the NEW Testament:

He gave them bread and drink, and He told them He was going to die. "I will bleed and die, so that you can be forgiven for all the wrong things you have done."

Later that night Jesus went out to a garden, and prayed to His Father. He was very sad.

- *Here's Something for Your Heart:* Jesus came to this world to love us and to help us.
- *And Here's Something You Can Pray:* Thank You, Jesus, for coming to love me and help me.

THE PASSION WEEK (Matt. 21:1-11, 26:20-30; John 12:12-19, 13:21-30) ■ **79**

JESUS SUFFERS AND DIES

While Jesus was in the garden, soldiers came to take Him. His friends all ran away.

The soldiers slapped Jesus, and hit Him with their fists. They tied Him up with ropes, and beat Him with a whip. They put a crown of sharp thorns on Him, and it cut His head. They spit on Jesus, and laughed at Him. Then they made Him carry a heavy wooden cross. On a hill, they nailed Jesus to the cross.

from the NEW Testament:

They also nailed two robbers to crosses, one on each side of Jesus.

On the cross, Jesus prayed to God. He asked God to forgive the men who hurt Him.

The sky became dark. Jesus prayed again to God, and then He died on the cross.

- *Here's Something for Your Heart:* Jesus died so that I can be forgiven for the wrong things I've done.
- *And Here's Something You Can Pray:* Thank You, Lord Jesus, for dying for me.

JESUS IS RISEN FROM THE DEAD!

Some friends of Jesus took His body down from the cross. They put it in a tomb that was like a cave. A big stone was rolled in front of the tomb. And soldiers stood guard outside it.

Three days later, early on a Sunday morning, the ground shook like an earthquake. An angel from God came down and rolled away the stone. Why? Because Jesus had risen, just as He had said! He was no longer dead.

from the NEW Testament:

A woman named Mary Magdalene came to the tomb. She saw that it was empty. She was afraid someone had taken away the body of Jesus. Then she saw Him! *Jesus was alive!*

Mary worshiped Jesus. Then she ran to tell His friends that she had seen Him.

- *Here's Something for Your Heart:* Jesus did not stay in His tomb. He rose up from the dead!

- *And Here's Something You Can Pray:* Thank You, Lord Jesus, that You are alive today and forever!

JESUS GOES BACK TO HEAVEN

Later that night, the friends of Jesus were
meeting in a room. The doors were locked.
Suddenly, Jesus was standing there with them!

His friends could hardly believe their eyes.
Was this really Jesus?

He showed them His hands and feet, where
the soldiers had driven in the nails. "Yes, it is
I," He said. "Touch me and see." Then they
gave Him some fish, and He ate it with them.

from the NEW Testament:

Jesus visited His friends again. "You will go all over the world to tell people about Me," He said. Then He lifted His hands, and began rising into the clouds, going back into heaven.

Suddenly two angels were standing there. "Jesus will come again someday!" the angels said.

- *Here's Something for Your Heart:* Jesus went back to heaven, but someday He will come again.

- *And Here's Something You Can Pray:* Thank You, Jesus, that You promised to come back to us.

Sharing Everything

One day Jesus' friends and all who believed in Jesus were sitting together in a house.

Suddenly the house was filled with a sound like a mighty wind. They saw what looked like tongues of fire resting above their heads. And now they talked about God in languages they had never spoken before.

God's Holy Spirit had come down to live inside them, to make them brave and good.

from the NEW Testament:

Many more people began to believe in Jesus
when they heard how He had died for them,
and had risen from the dead. They began
sharing their food and clothes and homes with
one another. And they came together to hear
more about Jesus, and to worship Him.

- *Here's Something for Your Heart:* God's Holy Spirit
  lives inside us to make us brave and good.
- *And Here's Something You Can Pray:* Thank You,
  God, for sending Your Holy Spirit to live inside us.

A BLINDING LIGHT

A man named Saul did not believe Jesus was God's Son. He hated people who loved Jesus.

One day Saul was on the road to Damascus. He was going there to find people who loved Jesus, so he could put them in jail.

Suddenly a light from heaven flashed all around him. Saul fell to the ground. Then he heard a voice from heaven: "Saul, why are you trying to hurt Me? I am Jesus."

from the NEW Testament:

When Saul opened his eyes, he could no longer see. The men with Saul led him by the hands into Damascus. God sent a man named Ananias to Saul. He put his hands on Saul—and Saul could see again! Now Saul knew that Jesus was God's Son, and Saul loved Jesus.

- *Here's Something for Your Heart:* Jesus can turn enemies into friends.
- *And Here's Something You Can Pray:* Lord Jesus, I love You, and I know You are God's Son.

AN ANGEL RESCUES PETER

Peter was in jail. The king put him there. The king was wicked. He did not like Jesus, and he did not like people who believed in Jesus. He put many of them in jail.

One night Peter was sleeping in jail between two soldiers. Suddenly Peter felt someone touching him. He woke up. It was an angel!

"Quick, get up!" the angel said. The chains fell off Peter's arms, and he got up.

from the NEW Testament:

"Put on your clothes," the angel said. Peter did. Then he followed the angel outside.

The angel left, and Peter went to the house where God's people were praying for him. He knocked on the door. When they opened it and saw Peter, they could hardly believe their eyes!

- *Here's Something for Your Heart:* God listens to the prayers of His people.
- *And Here's Something You Can Pray:* Thank You, Lord, for hearing my prayers.

SINGING IN JAIL

What would you do if you were in jail?

These two men were in jail, and they prayed and sang songs about God. One of them is Saul, whose new name was Paul. The other is Paul's helper, Silas. Paul and Silas were telling people about Jesus. They were beaten and put in jail by men who did not like Jesus.

While Paul and Silas were singing, there was a big earthquake, and their chains fell off.

from the NEW Testament:

The doors to the jail came open, too. Did Paul and Silas run out right away? No, they talked to the jailkeeper, who was very afraid. And what did they tell him? They told him about Jesus. Then the jailkeeper and all his family believed in Jesus, and they were happy.

- *Here's Something for Your Heart:* God can help us to praise Him at all times.

- *And Here's Something You Can Pray:* Help me to sing and pray, even when I am hurt.

Jesus Will Take Us to Heaven

Before Jesus died on the cross and rose again, He told His friends not to be worried. "I will go to heaven," He said. "Heaven has many big houses, and I will get all your houses ready for you. Then I will come back and take you to heaven to live with Me forever."

When Jesus comes back, we will hear a loud trumpet. Then we'll all meet Him in the clouds in the air. Won't that be wonderful?

from the NEW Testament:

Heaven is more beautiful than any place you've ever seen. Everything is always new in heaven. And everyone is always happy there. No one ever cries. No one ever hurts.

The best thing about heaven is that it is Jesus' home, and we'll live with Him there forever!

- *Here's Something for Your Heart:* Jesus wants us to live with Him in heaven, His wonderful home.

- *And Here's Something You Can Pray:* Thank You, Jesus, that You want *me* to live with You forever!

*"More desirable than gold...
and sweeter than honey..."*

That's what Psalm 19 says about Bible truths—
the same rich truths presented just for kids
in Questar's **GOLD'N'HONEY BOOKS:**

The Beginner's Bible
Timeless Children's Stories

The Early Reader's Bible
"I Can Read" Bible Stories

What Would Jesus Do?
IN HIS STEPS Retold for Children

The Beginner's Devotional

The Bible Tells Me So
*The Beginner's Guide to Loving
and Understanding God's Word*

My Best Bible Word Book Ever

The Beginner's
Bible Question & Answer Book

My ABC Bible Memory Book

The Bible Animal Storybook

The king of God's people said to David,
"But you're too little to fight Goliath!"

David answered,
"But if a lion tries to get
one of my father's sheep—
I go after him and kill him.
God protects me from the lion...
and He can protect me
from Goliath, too!"

from 1 Samuel 17:33-37